The Art of Selling Books

Books

A Sales Strategy for Authors

Ben Meeks

Sidestreet Publishing

Book Cover by Martin Shannon

1st edition 2024

Dedicated to Dino, The Patron Saint of Indie Authors

Contents

Foreword

Years ago, when I was a baby author without a clue, I happened to be at Dragon Con. One of the largest nerd conventions in the world, it has a track dedicated just to the craft and business of writing. Wanting to get an idea of just what all I didn't know (which was almost everything), I spent a lot of time in their panel room soaking up knowledge like a sponge.

I'd seen a lot of authors speak on these, but not once had I ever gone up after the panel to try and connect with them. Because after all, who was I? These were AUTHORS, and at that point I had no idea just how friendly and helpful authors usually are in the wild.

On one panel, however, there was an author who, when asked what it was he wrote, said 'I write about a were-otter hunting demons in the mountains of north Georgia.' I had never met someone writing southern urban fantasy like me, so I got over my shyness and approached him after the panel. And that was how I met Ben Meeks.

We started swapping emails, because like most authors, Ben is incredibly nice and helpful. In the years since we have developed a great friendship, and I consider him my closest friend in the 'biz.' As such, I would of course have written him a forward, no matter the book. But it makes me so happy that the foreword I am writing is for *THIS* book.

Because you see, Ben taught me pretty much everything I know about in person sales. I mean that. I had never done it before, and had no idea how to even start. But he took me under his wing, and over a number of events sharing tables, he showed me the ropes. If I learned it, and it didn't come directly from him, it came from me messing up and learning the hard way. Luckily for you, this book is going to let you skip the hard way if you take it to heart.

You may not know me, and you may have never had me sell you a book in the flesh. But I am regarded as a damn good seller by other authors I do events with. And it's all thanks to Ben. I watched him, following in his footsteps, and now am usually one of the higher selling authors at events where I'm a vendor.

And that's with selling weird little books about a meth wizard. If I wrote something even close to normal, using Ben's selling methods, I wouldn't have accepted his request that I write this forward when he messaged me. My people would have gotten back to him with a form letter, thanking him for his interest and that I 'would be in touch soon.'

I would intend to get back to him soon, but that amaretto sour out by the resort pool in Cabo wouldn't drink itself.

Hyperbole? Maybe a little. But I can honestly say that a large part of my success has come directly from what I have learned from Ben. And I am so, so glad that you are getting the same opportunity.

See you in the vendor hall!

-Bob McGough

Introduction

Not long after I published my first book, I realized it was hard to market. That wasn't surprising. It's a shifter urban fantasy book with no romance. If that wasn't enough, my main character is a wereotter. I was writing by passion and interest instead of writing to market. My problems were compounded by the fact that I was a new author that had no idea how to market my books.

Shortly after publication, I went to my first author event, The Dahlonega Literary Festival. I met Shanna Bosarge at the first panel I spoke on of my writing career. We became fast friends and chatted about social media, marketing, and sales. She had a regular event she sold books at and invited me to come along. Okay, I asked if I could come along, and she was gracious enough to take me. I went and the results... were lack luster. If memory serves, Shanna sold about fifteen. I only sold two.

I tried to wrap my head around what I was doing wrong. The only thing I knew was that I didn't have a pitch. Shanna had a script she would recite while I rambled about my book to anyone that would listen. While the pitch is important, I had a lot of other issues that were hurting me. Through a long trial-and-error process, I took what I learned from Shanna, expanded, and refined it. Eventually, fifteen to twenty book days at an event were the norm for me. Now, I give presentations on personal sales and this book is my way to pass on this knowledge to hopefully prevent the frustration and failure for you I went through.

This book isn't just a list of suggestions to improve your sales at events. It's a strategy. We're going to discuss how to find events, setting up a display that works, and how to engage a potential reader to make them want to buy your book. I'm going to talk about the principles of sales and how to apply them. You'll read some stories about real interactions I've had with prospective customers, both good and bad. By the end of this book you will be well on your way to being a pro at personal sales.

In person vs online sales

The best place to start a book about selling books in person would be to talk about why you would want to in the first place. We live in a digital world, after all, and you could potentially reach more people online, so why bother spending so much time selling books in person?

When I published my first book, I was hemorrhaging money. Online ads were expensive and didn't deliver the results I'd hoped for. I tried some online strategies that made profit but not much, especially considering how much time it took to put it all together. Without adds, sales were back and forth between miniscule and nonexistent. I made a decision that my writing was going to fund itself. That's a step I never hear anyone talk about. Authors that want a successful writing career focus on the dream of making a living, bypassing the steps that come between. The first step is publishing a book, the second is to have that book pay for your writing endeavors. It's possible. I know because I did it. Personal sales were the key to unlocking that vital step and what lead to leaving the career I had spent twenty years in pursuing writing full time.

The fact is the most profitable way for you to sell your book is in person. There's no middleman getting a cut. You can expect to make over twice as much for a book you sell yourself versus selling the same book online. With that kind of profit margin, it's easy to see how you can make money selling your books, if you do it right.

As technology progresses, the online space has become increasingly questionable. There are social media accounts with millions of followers from computer generated people. "Fake news" has become a common talking point. Online spaces are increasingly suspect, and people are becoming wary of them. Advertising is everywhere. It doesn't have the same impact it once did as the public becomes increasingly desensitized and apathetic. Any book marketing is an uphill battle but in person sales gives us the opportunity to bypass the hazard of the online space and develop human connections.

My Assumptions

For the purposes of this book, I'm going to make a few assumptions about you.

    1. You haven't done many (if any) events.

    2. Your catalog is small (one or two books).

    3. Your catalog will grow.

    4. You're a professional.

By professional, I don't mean that you make a living from your writing or even want to, rather, you have a professional mindset. You're putting out the best work you can. If you find a way to improve, you will implement it.

That leads us to the first and most important rule of book sales. What works for someone else might not work for you. Ultimately, it's going to take some trial and error to hone your skills and start making money. What you'll find in this book isn't a rigid set of rules that will work for some and not others. You will be able to use what you find here to tailor a personal strategy for success. I'm confident that with sound advice and practice, you'll be making a profit on your events in no time.

Part One: Events

Y ou might think finding events is a strange place to start instead of display set up and I agree with you. We're starting with events because there are a variety of events that you could do and some of them will take different equipment than others. You should consider what kind of events you want to do and how much money you're willing to put into a display to accommodate those events.

The first question you need to ask yourself is, are you interested in doing outdoor events? Some examples of outdoor events are fairs and festivals. In my hometown of Dahlonega, GA (pronounced DUH-lawn-uh-ga) there are multiple festivals every year. The largest, Goldrush, pulls in over 200,000 attendees to the quaint little mountain town. That's a lot of potential. One outdoor event I used to attend was an artisan market. It's little more than a parking lot in a high traffic area. It happens every Saturday all year long, so it's a great way to fill in the gaps between larger events. It was cheap and lasted five hours, so it didn't take up my whole Saturday.

Events like these can be profitable, but most don't supply anything but space. That means you will need to provide your own tent, tables, and chairs. Connecting to power isn't likely (more on this in the display setup section). That means they require more upfront capital to get into but can be just as (or more) profitable as indoor events.

Of course, all that extra equipment can be cumbersome. If you don't have a vehicle large enough to haul a tent, tables, and books, these events may not be an option for you. Another thing to keep in mind is weather. Events like this are often non-refundable. Some will say "rain or shine" as if people would be out shopping in the rain. This is really for the event promoter so they don't have to issue refunds if weather ruins the event. Heat and cold can also influence turnout but won't kill an event all together. The biggest issue is your personal comfort and the condition of your books. Paper and water don't mix. If you are at an outdoor event in the rain, even if the rain doesn't contact your books, the humidity alone can damage them.

Another consideration with outdoor events is they are open to the general public. You can't narrow down a target audience. My most profitable events are sci-fi/fantasy conventions. They are made up of my target audience and generally have large turnouts. The outdoor market was just people walking by, not my target audience. It made sales more challenging, but still worth it. If I wrote more mainstream genres like historical fiction or suspense/thriller, I would see better results at an event that caters to the general public. I encourage you to think outside of the box. Try to find events that will draw people that would be interested in your work but don't discount selling to the general public no matter what you write. The results may surprise you.

Where to Find Events

The internet is a great place to start. Check your local libraries and bookstores. Some ideas to search for are literary festival, book festival, festival of reading, Cons, and expos. If there is something in your book that might appeal to a certain kind of reader, try to figure out the kinds of events they like to attend. If you're writing a murder mystery where an angler is killed bass fishing and the only clue is a fancy lure found near the body, then a fishing expo might be a good event.

Another thing you can do is find authors that write in your genre and follow them on social media and check their websites for a list of where they will be. Authors will post events they're doing so this is a great way to find events that have probably been vetted. This is the easiest way to find events, but by the time you see them, it will probably be too late to participate.

There are also social media groups dedicated to author events. My favorite is a Facebook group called Author Events Around The World. Before you join a group you should be sure that they have, and enforce, a "no self-promotion" policy. I've found without this, a group devolves into constant *buy my book* posts and very few actual events. Do yourself a favor and steer clear. If you're in the southeast and write sci-fi/fantasy you should look at southernfan.com. The website lists conventions by month. With over twenty listings for most months, it's easy to find an event that caters to your target audience at a time that will work for you.

I encourage you to maintain a list of events you're interested in. Your list should include the dates of the event, when registration opens each year, and the registration cost. With that information, you'll be equipped to plan for the coming year and get your applications in early.

How to Choose Events

Regulations

The first thing to think about is what it takes to do business in the state you're considering. Some states require a business license and or tax registration to legally sell books at these events. You may also be required to file a tax return for the states you do business in. A professional author is a responsible business owner. That means getting your permits and paying your taxes where required. We will discuss taxes more in depth later. I suggest figuring out how far you're willing to travel. Research what's required to do business in those states and make your decisions on if it's worth it. A fine for operating a business without a license will likely make even the best event a waste of time. I have a six-state radius I am currently willing to work in. That list is slowly expanding. One of those states requires a Sales tax registration with the state and a business license that has to be displayed in the vending space. As of writing this, South Carolina is a state that requires registration for a sales and use tax account with the state and they enforce it. Agents showed up to a convention to check registrations and so few vendors had them that they closed the vendor hall entirely for the event. Do your research ahead of time and comply with the laws in the state where you're doing business.

If you only have one book, it makes the most sense to stay local and start cheap. The size of your catalog has a huge impact on how much you can make at an event. I didn't start including out-of-state events to my line up until right before I released my third book. I am skeptical that I will do events that I can't drive to simply because the logistics of transporting my display and books become much more problematic. With the extra costs of shipping books and equipment back and forth, it gets harder to make a profit the farther you go.

Artist vs. Vendor Spaces

Conventions have vendor spaces, sometimes called exhibitor spaces, but they may have artist or author spaces you could qualify for. The advantage of these spaces over a vendor space is that they're cheaper. You can expect them to be smaller than vendor spaces. While the standard vendor space is ten by ten, an author space could be six by ten, six by six, or even a single table in a hallway. This could be a good deal, but not always. The disadvantage is artist spaces tend to be a little out of the way. They are not necessarily in premium locations. If the vendors are all in a single room, you can expect the author spaces to be in the back of the room or in another location entirely. I attend Dragoncon every year. As the largest scifi/fantasy convention in the southeast, its vendor hall is four stories. The author spaces are on the top floor. I go to the vendor hall every year, but I have never made it up to the top floor. The takeaway is that while these spots are cheaper, they can also have less traffic. That's not necessarily a deal breaker, you'll need to run the numbers to make an educated decision on what would be best for your business.

Schedule

Events will book their spaces anywhere from three to nine months before the show. It's most common for booking to start around six months before. There are events you can just buy space at and be guaranteed a spot or there are juried applications. For juried applications it may take a few weeks or a few months to hear if you have been accepted. I've applied to events with juried applications and been booked for other events while I was waiting months to hear back. You need to decide how you want to handle this situation. Are you going to hold the weekend open once you apply and turn down other events or take the first event you can get into. Once you build solid relationships with other authors tell them to keep you in mind for sharing space in the future. If they are open to working with you when they find an event they will reach out to you about sharing and events start coming to you! The way I see it, an application is a show of interest. Nothing is official until money has changed hands. If I get another opportunity come my way, I'll take the sure bet over the possibility.

Next, consider the schedule. Are you going to be able to commit to the full event? Check the event dates and keep in mind that at larger events, load in may be done the day before. Load out will happen after it closes on the last day. There's only one thing I can think of worse than spending money on an event with a poor turnout. Unfortunately, poor turnout is just part of it. We're professionals, after all, and professionals stick it out. Don't leave before closing time unless the organizer stops by in person and tells you it's okay to pack it up.

If you decide to leave an event early, you better be sure you never want to do that event in the future. There's a good chance they won't have you back. Also, keep in mind that people talk. That one organizer from that lack luster event may have connections to more profitable events. If you show them you're a professional, you could get an invitation or accepted to better events. If you leave early, you may scratch your head at why your applications keep getting rejected.

What to look for

High traffic –

This system, and success in general, is predicated on having enough people around. It's the most important factor. If people aren't there, you can't sell to them. If it's a regularly occurring event, like the outdoor market I discussed above, then the event should pull in new people. You can only count on selling a book to someone once. Without a fresh crowd, you may do well the first time, but the second will be a dud. I'll try any event that looks promising. The ones I return to pull diverse crowds.

Shopping Mentality-

People should expect to spend money. I did an event once on a town square. There were plenty of people around, but they were all there on dates or had somewhere to be. The people there were too busy getting to where they were going to shop. They weren't there looking for a market, there was just a market there. In other words, they weren't shopping. I won't do an event like that again. Events at libraries can be hit or miss because of this. I've never had an exceptional sales day at a library, but I have made money. The nice thing about library shows is they are free to attend. This can be one factor when considering author spaces at conventions. The place to spend money at a convention is the vendor hall. If the author alley is in a hallway, attendees may be too busy getting to panels to stop and talk. They may not have a shopping mentality until they make a conscious decision to go to the vendor hall and see what's for sale.

Profitability -

I mentioned earlier that the second worst thing is to not have a crowd. The worst thing is to have a crowd and still not sell. How do you know if an event will pay off? If I'm being honest, there's no way to be one hundred percent sure. There are too many factors to consider. One mid-sized event I went to happened to be scheduled the same day as a sporting event close by. The events weren't related but people in the area had to decide what to do that day. The result was that my event didn't draw the expected crowd. I had no way to know about the conflict and I don't think I would have anticipated the impact if I did.

There is a lot of uncertainty and guess work in personal sales. For example, how many books should you take? After all, the last thing you need to do is pay for and lug around a bunch of inventory that doesn't sell. I've heard of lots of methods authors use to figure this out. Everything from take one book for every fifty attendees to just guess randomly.

I've developed a method to figure out how many books to take and what kind of profit you can expect to make from an event. I call it...

The Formula

Event time (in minutes) / Turnaround time = Reach

Reach / Sales Rate = Potential Sales

Potential Sales – 15% = Expected Sales

Reach

The way I see it, the most important factor when determining how profitable an event can be is not how many people are in attendance, but how many people you can talk to. Ninety-nine percent of the time, if you don't speak to someone, they won't buy your book. They probably don't even realize you're the author.

The first part of the equation covers how many people you can talk to.

Event time (in minutes) divided by turnaround time equals your Reach.

Event time in minutes: Look up how many hours you are able to sell at the event and multiple by sixty.

Turnaround time: The average time it takes to attract someone to your display and speak to them, sale or no sale. This should be around five minutes. Any less and you may be rushing and losing sales. More than this means you're spending too much with a potential customer. It's not a bad thing to get face time with a potential fan, but this system is designed to make money. You need to find a balance between quality and quantity of interactions.

Reach: the total number of people that you can speak to during the event. Reach helps you judge an event in relation to attendance. Any event you consider doing should be able to supply you with a steady stream of people, enough to fulfill your reach. If it can't, your sales will suffer.

Potential Sales

Reach divided by Sales Rate equals Potential Sales

Potential sales are the maximum number of sales you could expect to make for the event in question. Remember, if you don't speak to someone, you won't sell to them. Potential sales doubles as the number of books you should take to the event. You may be wondering why not use expected sales to determine how many books to take. The answer is, it's better to have books left over than to run out. The goal is to leave as little money on the table as possible. While you don't want to bring books home, they don't expire. You can always take them to your next event. If you run out, you're missing out on sales. It not only robs you of the profit from those sales, but the opportunity to make someone a fan and generate word of mouth. That far outweighs taking books home.

Sales Rate is the trickiest part of this formula. It is the average of how many sales you make out of how many people you talk to. Unfortunately, the only way to get hard numbers is from experience. Sales rate will be affected by how large your catalogue is, how appealing your display is, and how well you deliver your pitch.

If you have no experience or don't know where to start, I suggest one out of eight. That's 12.5%. If you feel confident in your pitch and display and you're at an event with your target audience, you could go as high as one out of five, 20%. These are starting out numbers.

As you build your selling muscles, you can expect to have higher sales numbers. My sales rate runs from one out of three to one out of five, depending on the event. Don't expect to have these percentages right out of the gate.

When you have a few events under your belt, you can divide Reach by the number of sales you have for that event to figure out what your sales rate is. Example: if you had a reach of sixty and sold fourteen books, that gives you over one out of four. 60/14= 4.29 Just shy of 25%. You can use that figure to calculate potential sales for that event and other events like it.

I need to note that this sounds misleading. I'm not saying that I sell a book to every third person I talk to. If I spoke to ten people and made one sale but that one person bought three books, then the average would be close to one out of three. This is how having a larger catalog makes events more profitable. If you only have one book to sell, your average could be considerably worse than with two or three books.

Expected Sales

Expected sales is exactly what it sounds like, the number of sales you are likely to make.

I take fifteen percent off the top of potential sales because things don't always go according to plan. Maybe your turnaround time was over five minutes, or you had to fit a couple bathroom breaks in, or the attendance wasn't what you expected. I hope you sell like crazy, but it's better to build a little buffer into the numbers. To get your expected sales, take your potential sales and multiply by .15. Subtract the result from potential sales. You'll use your potential sales number to determine if the event could be profitable.

Book Pricing

Let's take a second to talk about book pricing. It's common for a beginning author to undervalue their work. I was guilty of this too. When I published my first book, Petrified, I priced it at $9.99. Why? Because that's what I saw other books in my genre around the same length priced at. Of course, I was comparing to traditional published books in a large series. Not really apples to apples. I updated the cover, fixed some issues inside, and re-released it as a second edition. My new price was $14.99. I expect I could have gone as high as $17.99 without hurting sales. Why didn't I? Mainly, just so it would be easy to make change. I didn't want to have to go to events with a stack of ones. In the years since the second edition was released, I've gone back and raised my price again to $16.99.

If you're wondering how raising the price by seven dollars affected my sales, it didn't. My sales have increased since the price increase. The increase in sales isn't attributed to the price increase, of course. I've gotten much better at sales since then.

How you should price your book depends on what it is. If we're talking about a novel, you should be making at least ten dollars per sale. Look at your cost per book and triple it to get a starting idea. If that's not giving you at least ten dollars profit per sale, raise the price. For the examples of real events we will look at later on, we will assume ten dollars in profit per sale. This is not because I believe it's the magic number for profit, but because it makes math easy.

The Formula in Action

Now let's look at some actual events I researched. Let's run the numbers and see if they might be worth it.

Event one

Cost: $550(author space)

Selling hours: 34(2,040 minutes over four days)

Attendance: 80,000+

Reach: 408

Potential Sales: 82

Expected Sales: 70

This event is an enormous sci-fi/fantasy convention. I decided to go with the author space as the cheapest vendor space runs over eleven hundred dollars. I'm using a sales rate of twenty percent, one out of five, for this equation. I assume that if you're going to a convention like this, it will be your target audience.

The reach is 408. You can speak to, and have the opportunity to sell to, 408 people over the course of the event. The first thing to ask is; will this event have a steady stream of people, enough to allow you to meet your Reach? With over eighty thousand attendees, the answer is yes.

Next, we look at Potential Sales. That's how many books you should take. If your books cost five dollars each to print and ship to you, you will need to spend $410 to buy the eighty-two books on top of the $550 registration. Are you willing to put $960 into this event months before the event actually happens? That will depend on how much capital you have to work with and Expected Sales.

If you expect to sell seventy books at fifteen dollars each, your expected sales would be $1,050. So, you should make ninety dollars at the event, right? Not so fast. You need to eat and sleep. Let's assume you will need to find somewhere to stay close to the event. You'll need to pay for a hotel. You will also have travel expenses to consider. Plane tickets or gas and parking fees. If you're flying, you'll need to arrange shipping for your books as well. To make a profit you have $90 to work with. This event lasts for four days. Four days of eating out will run over $90 with no other expenses.

So, will this be a profitable event? The numbers say no.

Event Two

Cost: $100

Selling Hours: 5 (300 minutes from 7 PM to Midnight)

Attendance: Unavailable

Reach: 60

Potential Sales: 8

Expected Sales: 7

This is a market advertising "book related" items. They are trying to get authors but are open to anything author or book related. Since we can't guarantee our target audience, I'll be using the lower 12.5% (one out of eight) for these calculations.

According to the numbers, we should be able to speak to sixty people. We have eight potential sales but seven expected sales. With $40 in inventory and a $100 registration fee, we can expect to lose $35 on this event right off the top. Since it's a five-hour event we shouldn't have to worry about food and if it was close, no hotel, so travel expenses should be minimal. Did you notice the hours though? Seven to midnight. Who's going to be out buying books at midnight? No one. I doubt anyone will be out past nine. So, let's adjust our numbers accounting for two hours of good selling time.

Reach: 24

Potential Sales: 3

Expected Sales: 2

With our new numbers we can expect to sell only two books. With our expenses adjusted for the updated inventory we are likely to lose $85. Unfortunately, there are a lot of events out there like this. I'll stop short of calling it predatory. I will give the organizer the benefit of the doubt and assume they are attempting to put on a good event where authors have a chance to make some money. It's just not going to happen. Run your numbers and steer clear of events like this.

Event Three

Cost: $150

Selling Hours: 15 (900 Minutes over two days)

Attendance: No Data

This is a mid-sized author event. While we don't have an attendance number, from my research, I expect it to draw a good crowd. Like our previous example, I'll use the lower 12.5%(one out of eight) for these calculations.

Reach: 180

Potential Sales: 23

Expected Sales: 20

We see we can engage with 180 people during this event. We should take twenty-three books and expect to sell twenty. If the event is close by and we can pack lunch in, we won't have much to add in the way of expense. According to the numbers, we should be able to make about thirty-five dollars. This is an event I would consider doing.

Time Investment

Right now, you may be thinking; *You'd spend 9 hours to make $35? That's $3.89 an hour, not even minimum wage!* There's more to it than that. The truth is, there's more value in face time with readers than the amount of money you bring home. You'll have the opportunity to collect subscribers for your newsletter. You can generate word of mouth, which is the best advertising there is. In short, besides selling books, you will be building your brand. If readers like what you do, and want more of it, when you release your next book, you have a way to connect with people that will buy it.

It's not just about dollars and cents, it's about momentum. You start with a book and, hopefully, the support of your family and friends. You have a few reviews, but nothing to write home about. You take events where you can make a few dollars and that gives you the opportunity to build your business. The more you do, the more your fan base grows and the more connections you make. The larger your catalog and the better you are at connecting with readers, the more profitable these events become, the more word of mouth you generate, and it goes on and on to a successful writing career.

Increasing Profitability

Strategies for Upselling

If you only have one book for sale on the table, there's not much you can do. As your catalog grows, you can start bundling books to upsell. Upselling works best with a series but can be done with standalone books as well. Instead of one book at fifteen dollars, you can bundle two books for twenty-five dollars. The downside is you give up $2.50 in profit for each of the books sold. If you have three books, you could bundle all three for forty dollars. Now you're only losing $1.67 per book. If you write a series, you can increase profit even farther though by compiling your books into a single volume.

I took all the content for my wereotter series, *The Keeper Chronicles,* and bundled it into an Omnibus. It's three books and a short story, all the content for the series in a single volume. Let's look at the numbers of an omnibus. Let's assume, with proper formatting, you can get the omnibus for $7.50 each shipped. How much do you sell it for? At our example prices, the three individual books would cost us fifteen dollars to buy. If we bundled them with a five-dollar discount, we would make twenty-five dollars. If we stuck with this model and priced the omnibus at forty dollars, we would make $32.50 each sale. That's a big jump.

The trick is to add value for the customer. The price reduction works for this. Another strategy I used was to add the short story as well, so I can tell the reader it contains all the content for the series. The only way to get the short story is in the omnibus. I can also point out that they are saving five dollars to buy it all together. More content, less money. This strategy works. Most of my sales are the omnibus. If we only had one book and sold ten of them, we would make $100. With three bundled books, if we sold ten sets, we would make $250. If we sold ten omnibuses, we would make $325. That's a big improvement. It's easy to see how growing our catalog and packaging our books for upselling increases our profit.

Sharing Space: Teamwork Makes the Dream Work

Cutting your expenses in half is strikingly similar to doubling your money. The single best way to increase your profits is to share your vendor space with another author. It can be as simple as calling up your buddy who wrote that thing and inviting them along, but I urge you to consider an event partner carefully. Let's take an in-depth look at sharing space.

Selecting a Partner

There are some key factors I look for when finding an event partner. How successful they currently are, or how many books they have published, isn't a factor I consider. If you haven't built a wide list of author contacts, you may have limited options. That's not a bad thing starting out. When selecting a partner, I look for someone professional (there's that word again), cooperative, and amiable.

Like it or not, the person you are sharing space with is a reflection on you. A professional mindset, someone there to do business, is a must. Connecting with readers is the priority. It's fine to sit around and chat if things are slow, but you need someone that understands that when someone shows interest in your work, you're going to talk to them. It doesn't matter if your partner is in the middle of baring their soul about that awful thing that happened when they were eleven. You're going to put that conversation on pause and talk to the potential reader. You're both there to work. Socializing happens after the event.

In my experience, sharing space with someone doesn't hurt my sales, at least not noticeably. The exception to this is if you both write similar things. Another urban fantasy author isn't an ideal partner for me. I would, and do, still share space with them, but you will run into some people who will only buy one book from the table. If you write similar things, all other factors being equal, that person is going to pick whoever has the best pitch and presentation. As the event goes on, those one-book-buyers will gravitate toward the same person. If it's you, that's great, not so great for your partner.

Another pitfall is going it alone. With the right partner, I can increase sales over what I could do alone. This is done by working together. I'll get into this in depth in part three of this book. You don't want to get in a free-for-all mentality and try to outdo each other for sales.

Last but not least, you want someone amiable. This means finding someone that you can stand to be stuck behind a table with for hours or days on end. Someone that won't get their feelings hurt when you drop your conversation with mid-sentence to engage a potential reader. Someone who can at the same time be sad about their lack luster sales and be happy that you did better than expected, or vice versa.

Finding the perfect partner is nearly impossible, but most people who do personal sales understand these things and are generally a delight. None of this is anything groundbreaking, basic courtesy.

<u>Dos and Don'ts of Space Sharing</u>

I've shared space with a lot of people. I can honestly say I've only had one bad partner. I've had a few that do things that annoy me. Here are some tips to avoid annoying your partner.

<u>Unsolicited Advice</u>

Don't offer unsolicited advice or assume you know better. I have a personal policy on advice. I don't offer any unless I'm asked. Period. That's not writing specific, that's life in general. If you do ask, I'm going to tell you the truth so buckle up buttercup. I agree, it can be painful to see your partner making mistakes that are hurting their sales. That's on them. Keep your mouth shut... until they ask.

<u>Respect boundaries</u>

Generally, table etiquette is to split the space in half. They get one half, you get the other. Don't touch their side of the table. Don't take more than your assigned space. If you need more space and they have some they don't need, have that conversation but respect the boundaries.

I had a partner, good intentions aside, start to rearrange my display. Believe me, I've put a lot of thought into my setup and have things just the way I like them. They work for me. If you think you know better, that's great. Use that knowledge in your display and leave your partner's stuff alone.

<u>Equal Pay for Equal Play</u>

Once while sharing space at an event, a woman walks up out of nowhere and says, "What's the first book?" to my partner. My partner points out their first book. She buys it and leaves. My partner failed to mention that there was another "first book" on the table, mine.

I doubt the woman realized we were both authors. She didn't know anything about us or our work besides what she could see on the display. My partner did nothing to attract her attention or bring her to the table. In a scenario like this, the proper thing to do is provide full disclosure to the shopper. "We are both authors, and these are our first books." I've been speaking to a potential buyer and been interrupted mid-sentence by my partner to pitch their book. I've had a partner step in front of me, blocking me from view and preventing me from engaging. Don't be that person and don't work with people that consistently do these kinds of things.

You may think I'm talking about working together here. I'm not. That's still coming in Part Three. What I'm saying is we split the table fees. In the case of a walk up with a general question, the question should be answered to include everyone at the table. If costs are split evenly, then so should the opportunities. It's not uncommon for someone to buy books from both authors at a table, if they know there are two there and both have the opportunity to talk about their work.

Other products

Sometimes authors sell other things at their space. This can be a good way to increase profit, but this way lies danger. I've seen or heard of authors putting everything from 3D printed dragons to furniture and pillows for sale on their table. I saw one table that looked like a thrift store. The problem with this is that you run the risk of losing your author status. You don't want to be a furniture seller who happens to have a book, You're an author first. Everything you're selling should relate to and support that goal.

James Maxey, a multi series fantasy author, struck a balance with this. He shares vendor space with his wife, Cheryl. She knits Octopuses (Octopi?), dragons, and other creatures that she sells on one side of the space. He does his author business on the other. This is a great way to do it because they get the added income from her knitted creations, but his author brand remains intact.

When my youngest daughter was eleven, she came into my office and said, "I need money. What can I do to make some money?" I'm not one to discourage and entrepreneurial spirit, so we went to work figuring out something she could do. We looked at a lot of options but settled on a soap business. After investing in the equipment and doing the research, she was off to the races. We shared space at my market events. My sales weren't hurt, and she was raking in some profit, often bringing home more than I did.

Since this is my livelihood, adding another product to increase profit is an appealing proposition. I thought about what I could do for a while before I remembered the soap. I had all the equipment and knowledge. It's a minimal time investment, but I didn't want to be a soap vendor who, by the way, has some books too. No, I'm an author. If I was going to do it, I would need to tie the soap into my work somehow. I could name the fragrances after characters from my books. The idea being, if someone walks up interested in soap, I can't help but talk about my books in the process of selling them soap. The integrity of my author brand is maintained. This is an extreme example since soap and books don't really align. If you have another talent or product you can make, think about how you can tie it to your books.

I'm not suggesting you learn new skills and shell out for equipment to have another product. Most authors who have day jobs trying to kick off a writing career don't have the time to manage another product line. There's nothing wrong with that. If there is some low hanging product fruit that you could do, it might be worth it. Whatever it is, remember, you're an author first. All products should lead back to your books.

That brings us to an interesting side note, You don't have to share space with another author. Any vendor could potentially pay off. You will come to know and build relationships with authors, so they tend to be the easiest people to find to share space with. The most common second runner-up is artists. Be open if an opportunity for sharing spaces arises.

Sharing the Love: Space Sharing with Multiple People

The next logical step in this progression is if you can make so much more sharing with one person, then sharing with more people means you would boost your profit even higher, right? Well, not so fast. I mentioned earlier that splitting the table with one person won't noticeably affect your sales. Having more than two people in the space will. The reason is you can easily work with one person. Both of you can pitch to the same people. With more people, it becomes increasingly difficult to speak to every customer. You can't expect to speak to someone and pass them on to three other people. They aren't interested in standing around being pitched to all day.

With three or more people, those other authors standing right beside you will effectively reduce your reach. If the crowd is large enough, you can theoretically overcome this obstacle, unless the customers the other authors are talking to stand in front of your space. Table obstruction is an issue, not just when sharing space. Even when you're on your own, it's rare that you will have a walk up while you are speaking to someone. The reason is simply the person standing in front of your table blocks the view of your display. If your neighbor pulls in a family or group shopping together, they can take up the space in front of your display. There just won't be space for you to do business with them standing in front of you. You'll have to wait for that author to pass them over to you to pitch, assuming they do.

In these situations, it's not uncommon for the author that got their attention first to keep it until they finish the interaction before throwing in a "By the way, there are other authors you might like here as well." At that point, it tends to be too late. They've already heard a pitch and wrapped up their business at the table.

On top of that, fitting multiple people into a ten-by-ten foot space is problematic. Only three people fit in a ten-foot display space and then it can be cramped. The best way to get around it? Pay more for one of the premium corner spaces or get two spaces. With a corner you have two faces of your space accessible customers instead of one. Adding another space doubles your event fees, but you have twice the space. Both options increase your costs, which offset the savings from sharing space in the first place.

While adding more people to the space can reduce costs further, it will also cut into your sales. I'm not saying having four people in a space wouldn't be worth it. I'm saying things get considerably more complicated. Do I foresee a time when I should split a corner space with three other people? Absolutely, but it has to be the right, meaning very large and very expensive, event. Consider splitting the hotel in this scenario as well. I don't know about you, but I'm not a young buck anymore. Sharing a hotel with three other people can be questionable. I will not be sleeping on floors or on a cot to save a few dollars. My back can't take it and I need to be in top shape for a day of sales. I do have a hammock with a frame I use for these situations that sleeps well. Cutting costs in thirds could be a good option, even with reduced sales. With that in mind, I'm going to repeat myself again. Run the numbers, consider the pros and cons, and see if it's something you're willing to do.

Working together with groups

While sharing with a group can hurt your profit, it doesn't mean that you can't work together. It's just harder. To do this, when you get a customer at the table, ask them what they like to read. Then direct them to the author with the closet book. If you're going to try this, you need to think outside of genre. For example, I have a 100% success rate with people that say they like R.A. Salvatore. The Keeper Chronicles is very similar. Action packed fantasy with cruel matriarchal elves. My books are Urban Fantasy while Salvatore's are high fantasy. So, if I'm sharing with someone that writes a high fantasy romance, based on genre alone it would make sense to send that reader to the high fantasy author even though the book may not have the things they like about Salvatore's high fantasy. The authors need to understand each other's work so they can refer people to books that are the best fit.

Space Sharing's Effect on Profit

Speaking of numbers, let's look at how sharing space would affect the profitability of two of our events above. I'm leaving out event two, its hot garbage.

Event one

Solo

Cost: $550

Inventory Cost: $410

Expected Sales: $1050

Expected profit: $90

<u>Two People</u>

Cost: $225

Inventory Cost: $410

Expected Sales: $1050

Expected profit: $315

<u>Three People</u>

Cost: $366.66

Inventory Cost: $275

Expected Sales: $750

Expected profit: $108.34

<u>Four People</u>

Cost: $275

Inventory Cost: $275

Expected Sales: $700

Expected profit: $150

If we share with one person, we split the cost of the space in half, $225. None of the other figures change so that bumps our expected profit from $90 to $315. That's a big difference! Remember, this is a four-day convention. That means travel and food costs should also be included in your equation. Your new partner will need a hotel as well, so why not share a room? By adding the savings of a hotel room as well, you're looking at some serious savings. Will it be worth it? That depends how much those travel expenses are, but it will definitely be more reasonable. I should say that in this scenario, the amiability of your partner is even more important. Sharing a table and a hotel means you will spend close to four days straight with this person. It's easy to see how someone hard to get along with could turn the trip into a nightmare. It's another thing to consider in your cost/benefit analysis.

For the three and four person numbers, I had to upgrade the space, which increased the cost. In the original example, the space was in the author's ally, a single six-foot table. To accommodate three or four people, we have to upgrade to a vendor hall space. For four people, we should really consider a corner space which would be more expensive, but for this example, I assume we found a way to make the normal ten by then work. I reduced the inventory cost and the expected sales to account for the competition additional authors provide. As you can see, it becomes more difficult to make a profit when taking all these factors into account.

Event Three

<u>Solo</u>
Cost: $150
Inventory Cost: $115
Expected Sales: $300
Expected profit: $35
<u>Two People</u>
Cost: $75
Inventory Cost: $115
Expected Sales: $300
Expected profit: $110
<u>Three People</u>
Cost $50
Inventory Cost: $100
Expected Sales: $210
Expected profit: $60
<u>Four People</u>
Cost: $37.50

Inventory Cost: $90

Expected Sales: $180

Expected profit: $52.50

Splitting the cost in half takes our registration fee down to $75 and raises our profit to $110. While you scoffed at the paltry $3.89 an hour before now, we're looking at $12.22 an hour. Much better, with the same branding and reader connection. Maybe you're scoffing at the $12.22 as well. I'll refer to Assumption One; you're new at this. It gets better.

I've played eight holes of golf in my entire life. I would hit the ball and it would bounce toward the hole. No airtime whatsoever. I was getting frustrated. I didn't care so much if it flew toward the hole, I just wanted to get some air. The gentleman I was playing with saw me getting frustrated and commented, "What?! You want to play perfect golf your first time out? Are you an idiot?" His bluntness aside, his comment is applicable here. Don't expect to be good at things when you're starting out. Have reasonable expectations.

We hypothesized that this was an event close by with no hotel expenses and no food costs, since we packed a lunch. Where I said before it was an event I would consider doing, with these updated numbers I absolutely would participate.

With three or four people in the space, we end up losing money compared to a two-way split with the adjusted numbers. That's assuming we could fit them in the space to begin with. Why would you want to consider a three-way split when overall it's not as profitable for you? One reason is, it's cheaper to get into. If you're tight on funds and the only way to be at the event is sharing with a group that might be better than not going at all.

Free Events

If the event you're looking at has a writer's track, you can apply to participate as a speaker. This means paneling or lecturing, if you have an expertise you feel comfortable speaking about alone. Paneling is the most common. I recommend sitting in on panels to begin with and after you get comfortable, you can start moderating. The good news is you can often get cheap or free table space for taking part in the event. The table spaces that are provided will be in the "author alley." These spaces aren't always secured overnight, so you may have to pack in and out every night if you aren't comfortable leaving your inventory in a public place overnight. Free spaces are great though, especially if you're starting out or short on cash to pay for spaces.

Concerning Theft

There's an Iraqi proverb that says, "The reader doesn't steal and the thief doesn't read."

I don't personally know of anyone who has had a book stolen at an event. I've spoken to a few authors about this and the consensus seems to be if someone steals a book, they really needed it. There are other things people can steal besides books. Your cashbox for example. At Dragoncon 2023, one of the vendors in the vendor hall had their cashbox stolen, losing thousands in cash. If you have other items on your table, either for sale or as part of your display, you might want to consider how likely it is they might disappear and what the implication would be. I have some small book related items on the table that I have caught kids trying to walk off with a few times. I tried stickers out, a common author accessory, and people stole those regularly, not just kids. These small items don't have a large price tag and have no impact on my bottom line, so it isn't a big deal. Another item I have on my table is hand turned pens. It's a hobby I picked up a few years ago. With pens piling up in the house, I started putting them on the table as an extra. The price tag ranges from twenty-five to eighty dollars for most pens. If these grew legs, it would be a different story. I haven't had any issues but keep them on the table in the most secure location I can. There seems to be a small but passionate group interested in fancy pens, so most people don't pay any attention to them.

If it's a multi-day event, people leave their displays set up with inventory in their space overnight. I do this as well, but I take anything valuable or irreplaceable. My pens, petty cash, square, and tablet come with me when I leave for the day. Everything else gets covered by a spare tablecloth and left behind.

Investing in Loss

Sometimes the numbers won't show a profit and you should go anyway. I don't think you should regularly do events that lose money, but there are a lot of networking opportunities, especially at large conventions. Networking can open a lot of doors. You will start to see and make friends with the same people from event to event. Don't be afraid to ask them about what events are worth doing. People that have been doing it for a while will have a good idea of what the best events are. There are other opportunities that may present themselves as well. Recently, I was invited to write books for an officially licensed game world. Make friends with the authors around you, get their business cards, and friend them on social media after the event. Networking is one of the most important things you can do at events.

Part Two: Display Setup

The Necessities

I have good news! We're done with math. Now that you have an event, or at least know what you're looking for, it's time to turn your attention to setting up a display that works. In part one, I spoke briefly about the equipment needed to do outdoor events. Beyond that everything else is the same so I won't mention the outdoor vs indoor equipment here. A successful display will work for both.

There are three things I feel strongly enough about to be non-negotiable. The first is this; In my opinion, there are three things you must have, besides books, to have a successful display. A tablecloth, bookstands, and a way to take payments. I take a hard stance on this. If you don't have all three, don't bother showing up. Assumption Four, you're a professional. That is the bare minimum for a professional-looking display. The good news is you shouldn't have to spend a lot to get these things. Let's take a more in-depth look.

Tablecloth

The most common table size you will encounter is eight feet long, so if you're only going to have one tablecloth, two if you want to cover your display overnight, get an eight footer. It should be black. I have no idea what your books look like or what colors are on the cover, but I do know they will look good on a black cloth. Whatever books you release in the future, no matter what design or colors they use, they will look good on a black tablecloth. If it ain't broke, don't fix it.

Your tablecloth should go all the way to the floor. Standard tables are twenty-nine inches tall and thirty inches wide so you should look for a tablecloth at least sixty inches wide to cover the top and front of the table. While you're at an event, the space under your table doubles as your stockroom. It will let you keep your space clean and the mess out of sight. In the event you find yourself with a six-foot table, you can fold the cloth under itself to make it fit or use binder clips to crimp the edges.

Book Stands

You need some way to display your book. It doesn't have to be fancy. You can find a pack of wire bookstands for less than swinging through a drive through. All they need to accomplish is to hold your book facing your customers. I've seen several people new to sales events that put a stack of books on the table and prop one up against them. If the cost of a bookstand is prohibitive, it's a viable option, but it ain't classy. You've put a lot of work into your book. It deserves to be displayed properly. You can't expect anyone to take your work more seriously than you do.

Taking Payments

If you're wondering how many people pay with cash, on average, about fifteen to twenty percent. I've seen as high as fifty and as low as zero. A way to take payments means two things. You will need some change for cash transitions, and you will need a point of sale (POS) system. The most popular POS system authors use is Square. There are other payment systems out there you can use, like PayPal and Clover. Personally, I use Square. They are upfront about the fees they charge and if you sign up, they will send you a free card reader to use with your phone. As of writing this, the connections on the card reader are out of date. For Android it uses a headphone jack and iPhone uses a Lightning connector. I hope they will upgrade to a USB-C connection soon. You may need to get an adapter to use them with modern phones.

Since I do a lot of events per year, I paid to upgrade to the chip reader with the tap feature. It connects via Bluetooth, so it's universal. It's a much nicer system to use and in the case of disputes, you have added protection by using a chip reader. That's not a big concern for me. In the years I've been doing this, I have never had, or heard of, anyone with a payment dispute for a book sale. I upgraded because it's a more reliable system and checkout is much faster.

There are other payment systems I've seen people use, like Venmo or Cashapp. I suspect they do this to try to avoid transaction fees. Some authors have a QR code to their preferred app on their table for people to use. This is fine in most cases but be aware that some of these services are for personal transactions only and have upgraded services for businesses. Violating terms of service isn't a very professional thing to do and if they catch on, you could find your account suspended in the middle of a sales day. This could be a major inconvenience if you're using it as a primary method of payment. Besides that, you don't want to lose sales because you don't have a payment option a customer can use. It's our job to make paying easy for our customers.

If you're interested in getting a square, here is a referral QR code. We would both get rewards when you sign up and process your first transaction. You can select a twenty-dollar discount from the square store to purchase a chip reader or square will wave up to one thousand dollars in transaction fees for 180 days.

You will need a device to use the square with and an internet connection to process payments. Some venues will allow you to connect to their internet. I would recommend the device you use has its own internet connection. I've found it more reliable to use a 5G connection than to connect to someone else's internet service. Your phone is an obvious choice. Starting out, stick with your phone. I have a tablet I use for checkout. I'm not draining my phone's battery processing sales. The tablet has 5G with a data plan. Besides using it for checkout, I have my newsletter signup saved as an icon, so it's easy to access. Since I do a lot of space sharing, it's nice to have a separate device to handle checkout. It's always set up on a stand ready to go. If I go to a panel, I don't have to leave my phone behind. My partner, who is hopefully pitching my book, can ring up sales. A tablet is a good choice for this because, like a phone, it can be charged from a battery. The downside is the extra cost involved in having another device.

Extras

Your display is an extension of your personality. I like my space uncluttered and everything in its place. If you want to see some images of my space, look me up on social media. Facebook or Instagram user authorbenmeeks. I'm always posting pictures from events. If you do take a look, you will notice my display is consistent. I have only one bookstand per book facing front. As of writing this, I have four books to display and will have seven displayed on the table. I keep two or three of my top sellers stacked behind the stand, just so I don't have to go fishing in my bins after every sale. That's what I like. If you only have one or two books, I urge you to not put too many on the table. As a beginning author with a small catalog, too many books on the table could send a message to shoppers. No one's buying. If people were buying, then you obviously wouldn't have so many, right?

I don't know the psychology behind it, but I have an idea. I call it the Chump Theory. It goes like this. There you are, a brand new author with their first book. You have a customer looking at it and they're on the fence. It sounds interesting, but they know it's your first book. How good could someone's first book be, really? They haven't heard of or seen anyone buying your book. If they buy it and it's awful, then they've been made a fool of, a chump. No one wants to be a chump, so the safe thing to do is pass on the book.

That's another reason it's so important as a beginning author to present yourself as a... know what I'm going to say? Professional. As your catalog expands, this problem shrinks. If you have eight books in your catalog, you obviously have had success and know what you're doing. You will naturally have more books on the table because you have more books to display.

You can get more books on the table by having one stand displaying the front of your book and another displaying the back. Even though you're displaying the same book, it's not the same display. Until I released my second book, I put five books on the table. Two in a stand with the front displayed, two in a stand with the back displayed, and one flat on the table to be picked up and flipped through. When I released the second book in the series, I just added one stand with two facing front, bringing my total books displayed to seven.

Another reason for keeping fewer books on the table is that it can create a sense of urgency for the buyer. If it looks like you don't have enough to go around, they may be enticed to get their copy when they can, before you run out. We don't have to disclose that there's another twenty copies under the table. I've had people ask if I had more books, because they wanted one but didn't want to carry it around while they shopped. I always tell them the truth, I have plenty. I'm not saying you can't put more books on your table, it is your table after all, but sometimes less is more.

You will have people that will say they will come back and buy it. Most of the time, they don't. I'm not saying they're lying, maybe they meant to and forgot, or had an emergency. Whatever happens, if they leave the table without a book, don't expect to see them again. They're in the wind. If they really wanted your book, you can't expect them to remember your name or be able to find it from an internet search. Which leads us to the second thing I feel strongly about.

Business Cards

You need a business card. Many beginning authors I see don't have a business card. Many opt for bookmarks instead, or even postcards. You need something to pass out to people with your information on it. If they don't have your information, they can't look you up later. Everyone I speak to gets a card, even if they express no interest in my book. Even if they say they hate fantasy and otters and reading. I pass out thousands of cards a year. When they're about to leave, I hold one out and say, "Let me give you a card if you want to check it out later or you know someone who might like it." I want to plant the seed in their mind, get them thinking of who they know that might like my work. If I'm lucky, they pass the card along and whoever they give it to will look me up. It works. With no online advertising, only doing in person events, I regularly have online sales and Kindle Select reads. That success comes from business cards.

So why not a bookmark? You can put the same information on them as a business card and after all, how neat is it to have a bookmark for your book, right? Simple. Bookmarks are cost prohibitive. A business card will run you about four cents each. A bookmark will cost thirty-seven cents. That's almost ten times the cost. To prove my point, let's look at the three events from earlier, without sharing space. I'll multiply the cost of each by our reach, because everyone we speak to gets one. Then we will compare the costs to the expected profit.

Event One
Business Cards $16.32
Bookmarks: $150.96
Expected Profit: $90
Event Two
Business Cards: $.96
Bookmarks: $8.88
Expected Profit:-$85
Event Three
Business Cards: $7.20
Bookmarks: $66.60
Expected Profit:$35

As you can see, giving a bookmark to everyone you talk to will make every event a loss. So, if that's all you have, it doesn't make sense to give them out to everyone. How will you determine who gets one? The answer to that is only people that buy your book would get one because you can't afford to give them to anyone else. The people that buy your book are the ones that need your information the least. They already have it from your book. It's your money, do what you want with it, but if your goal is to make a profit and build your business, you need a business card.

If you take my advice and decide to get some cards, let's talk about what you should have on them. A traditional business card will have the business name, the persons name, phone number, and maybe an address. They are just a way to give someone your information. That's well and good, but for our purposes, what we're really looking for is an advertisement. We want to entice the people that we've given the card to, or the people they've passed it along to, to check out our work. If that's a goal, basic information won't cut it.

You know what makes a great bookmark? A business card. With that in mind, I like to orient my business cards vertically. On the front I put artwork. We're going to talk about artwork later in this section. For now, let's assume you'll use your book cover. That leaves the space on the back for everything else. You need to have your website and social media at least. An email wouldn't hurt. In the space left over, you have some options. You could put a couple of sentences from a book review or two. You could use a QR code to the landing page on your website. If you're going to use a QR code, I recommend setting up a Linktree account. Linktree will let you put all the links you want into a single QR code. In my Linktree, I have links to my website, amazon author page, newsletter signup, and social media accounts. One link to rule them all. Whatever you decide to put on your card, keep in mind that it should encourage anyone who sees it to look into your work.

Newsletter Signup

You should have a newsletter signup on your table. At first, I made a QR code for people to sign up with. No one used it. I changed to a sheet of paper on a clipboard. I still have the QR code on the top of the sheet, just in case. This works much better. One thing I like about it is that I can keep the same sheet with signatures on it until the sheet fills up. It's helpful to have signups on the sheet to show customers that people are signing up. The downside is people have sloppy handwriting and it can be difficult to figure out what their email address is. When someone signs up, check the email address and make sure you can read it. If you can't ask them what it is before they leave. I have a link to my newsletter signup saved on my tablet and sign them up right away. If I can catch them before they start writing, I will hand them the tablet and have them enter their own information there instead.

If you aren't getting many signups, you could offer an incentive. A one-dollar discount off the price of your book is a good way to go. Other options might be a complementary bookmark. Bookmarks are cheaper than a dollar discount in this scenario. If you offer an incentive, it should be something small and inexpensive. Just because someone signs up for your newsletter doesn't mean they will stay signed up. They could unsubscribe as soon as they leave your table. You should stay away from percentage discounts on your books. You would have to offer somewhere in the five to ten percent range to get the desired affect but that could end up costing you a lot of money in the long run.

If you have a reader magnet, that could be enough incentive on its own. I have offered incentives in the past and found them unnecessary. Just having the sheet on the table with a pen on it does the trick. Also, you have to tell everyone about the incentive for it to work, which ends up being another thing we need to think about in our interactions with our customers.

Artwork

Adding artwork to your display can be a great way to attract attention. When I released my first book, the standard was a foam board poster. I'm not a fan of these. They are easy to damage and need something to lean against or require a tripod to use them. A better option is a retractable banner. They have a spring-loaded roller in an aluminum case. When traveling, the artwork rolls up inside the case and stays protected. They have collapsible poles that slide into the frame. The banner pulls out of the frame and hooks onto the top of a pole. A "table top retractable banner" will cost around $25. The larger floor model starts around $125. That's not including the cost of the artwork if you decide not to use your cover.

Most authors I see use their book covers to make banners and posters out of. I'm not a big fan of using book covers as display materials. I get it, artwork is expensive. The thing is, your book cover is already represented on the table on the front of your book. I don't think making it larger adds anything. If you are going to use the artwork from your cover, consider changing the graphics on it to make it a unique promotional piece. That can be done for a fraction of the cost of new artwork and isn't redundant. If you're reading this to get a better understanding of book sales but don't plan to do many events, it's probably not worth the expense to add a banner to your display.

If you're writing mainstream genres like historical fiction or mystery/suspense you probably don't need a banner at all. I think banners really help with sci-fi and fantasy. It gives you the opportunity to show some of the cool things that are unique to your story and attract people interested in those things. The banner I use features three of the main shifters in my story. My main character the wereotter, his apprentice a weredoberman, and his best friend, a werebear that runs the shifter motorcycle club the Tortured Occult. I have the series name, THE KEEPER CHRONICLES, in bold letters. It gets a lot of looks. If you're wondering what effect it had on my sales, they improved by one third, immediately.

I contribute the increase in sales to two factors. One, it just attracts attention which helps me meet my reach goal. Two, the idea of a wereotter is a foreign concept to most people and many don't know what that means. By having a picture of a wereotter it helps solidify the concept. Before the banner I would get asked all the time what a wereotter is. Now I've built into my pitch that when I say 'wereotter' I point to a picture of Obie, they look at the picture, and they get it. Consider what characters or unique things about your book might attract people to your work.

A good idea for a banner would be to put your picture on it and words declaring you are the author. 'Meet Author Ben Meeks!' or 'Author Ben Meeks Book Signing.' Most people don't realize that the person behind the table could be the same person who wrote the books. Paige Christie took this one step further. Her banner is set up this way with a wooded backdrop. She printed out copies of her covers and affixed magnets to the back so she can change the banner depending on the event and which books she would like to promote. It's a great idea if you write in multiple genres.

<u>Signage</u>

I'm a big supporter of displaying the price of your book. Don't get me wrong, even with my price displayed, the most common question I get is, "How much is it?" I made a sign with my series name, my name, the prices, and a QR code that goes to my amazon author page. If you want a QR code on your table that goes to Amazon you should send it to your amazon author page because the address doesn't change and it lists your full catalog. Again, no one uses QR codes but when I get asked if it's available in ebook, I can point to the QR code and say, "It sure is, I have a QR code right here to get it on amazon." Another idea is a sign about you. A picture with your author bio on it. This is a good alternative to a banner.

You don't have to use expensive signs in your display. You can print out signage and put it in an 8x10 black picture frame supported by an extra book stand. Simple, cost effective, and gets the job done.

I've also seen and experimented with digital signage. By that I mean using a computer monitor or tablet to display images and information. I would advise the beginning author to keep it simple and stick to picture frames. Digital signage requires power and technical expertise to set up. Not all events have access to power and the ones that do often charge more to hook up to it. Also, digital signage becomes unreliable outside. If you're facing the sun can make it hard to see. You could use a tablet for digital signage and run checkout on the same device. I've tried this and found it to be cumbersome to constantly be switching between the two.

Another option is to put a sign on the top of your books with attention-getting phrases. Bob McGough writes *The Redemption of Howard Marsh* series about a redneck wizard from Alabama with a crippling meth addiction. He has an index cards he puts in the top of his books. One of them says, "If Harry Dresden did meth!" It was from a review a reader left for him. People walk by, read this, and then come up to ask him about it. This is a great way to attract attention to your work.

<u>Batteries</u>

While I wouldn't pay an up charge to have access to power, I do have a battery in my supplies. If the device you use for checkout dies, you're out of business. A battery backup is good insurance. Since I have the square chip reader, I keep it and my tablet plugged into my battery during selling hours. The Square doesn't go to sleep when it's plugged in, so I don't have to constantly reconnect it. The battery I have is 10,000 mAh, enough to run my electronics for a long weekend without recharging. It's close to the size of a brick. If I needed to, I could charge my phone as well. I actually have two batteries, the second one is still substantial but not nearly as powerful as my main battery. At one event, my neighbor left their battery at home. I lent him my smaller battery for the weekend. Don't spend money on extras you don't need but if you find yourself at an event in need of power ask around to see if someone can help you out. If I'm there, come talk to me. I got you covered.

Batteries can be expensive, but it's one of the best additions you can make to your booth. You don't need to shell out a lot though. A much smaller battery than the two I have would work fine, if you charge it overnight for a multi-day event. Once you have your battery, don't forget the cables you will need to charge your devices.

<u>Transporting Your Books</u>

Many authors transport their books in the boxes they were shipped in. I don't recommend this. I went to an event as a new author and during the car ride, my box of books jostled in the back of the car. When I opened the trunk, the books fell out into the dirt. Many of them were torn or muddy from the puddle they landed in. I lost a third of the inventory I had on hand from that tumble. Ever since I have been looking for the perfect book bin. This bin would fit six by nine books snuggly in a single or double row, have smooth plastic, and a weather sealing lid that clips on. I've come to the conclusion that the perfect bin for transporting books doesn't exist. It is still worth springing for a bin as close to those specifications as you can find. The trouble is, most bins slant inward toward the bottom or have plastic tabs jutting out around the edges that can damage books.

If it's made out of a rough plastic, most of the time black instead of clear plastic, your books can get scuffed up during transport. If you settle on a bin like this, you can make a cardboard insert to protect your books from the plastic. I stack my books with the spines and covers facing inward, away from the plastic to ensure minimal scuffing on the most important sides. Most of the time, the backs of books aren't displayed. I also put my tablecloth on top of the books, so I don't have to worry about them getting damaged by the tabs on the lid if they take a tumble. Don't trust the inside dimensions given online. If you can see the bin in person, take a couple books to see how well they will fit in different orientations.

Whatever bin you choose, remember to consider how heavy it will be when it's full of books. I've used some very large bins that were hard to move around when they were full. Now, I've moved to smaller bins to make moving and carrying them easier.

Speaking of moving bins, you might need a cart to make transporting your equipment easier. I see a lot of authors use collapsible wagons. They are cost effective and get the job done. I opted for the "8 in 1 multi cart" design. They have a higher weight capacity and are easy to maneuver but might be overkill for someone starting out.

Another option I have become very fond of is a modular toolbox. This is what I use for most events. I have a large bin with wheels on the bottom. It holds all my equipment for the event. A medium-sized middle bin holds my books. I lined it with cardboard to protect the books from the plastic. I can fit enough books to cover a single day, no matter how busy it is. The top bin is smaller. I keep my bags and cash in it as well as anything else I need easy access to. If it's a multi-day event, I can put all my valuables in the small bin and use the handle to carry it out for the night.

The system I use is a Rigid Pro Gear 2.0. I have spent more hours than is reasonable researching modular toolboxes and determined this one to be the best to suit my needs. One of my favorite things about this system is that the wheels are removable from the bin. This means if I'm doing a very large event that requires more equipment, I can leave the wheels at home and take the bins in on my cart with the other gear I need. If I need more books, I can add another medium bin to the stack and roll them all in together. It's also backwards compatible with the first-generation Rigid boxes. The first generation has a cooler that makes bringing in lunch and drinks easy.

<u>Everything in Your Space is Part of Your Display</u>

You don't want to have anything or anyone in your display that will distract someone from your pitch. If you have to take your disgruntled teenager, who's upset about being dragged to some dumb book thing, that teenager is part of your display. You're part of the display too. I'm not going to insult you by going over hygiene and cleanliness, you know all that. I do what to talk about clothing. You're going to have to speak to a lot of strangers, so dress comfortably. By comfortable, I mean not only comfortable to wear but what you are comfortable in. If you're self-conscious, you probably won't pitch well. The first time I gave the presentation on sales that inspired this book I put on a polo and stood in the bathroom mirror checking my appearance. I looked at myself and said, "I don't even know who you are anymore." If you ever see me selling or speaking at an event, I'll be wearing a tee shirt or sweatshirt. Even in a polo, I feel self-conscious. I don't dress up unless I have to.

Keep in mind that the temperature inside may not be what you expect. It often gets cold in vendor halls, especially if it's hot outside. The venue turns down the air conditioning to accommodate all the people and the result is a chilly room. I take a long sleeve tee and a hoodie so I can add or remove layers to stay comfortable.

<u>Flair</u>

Some authors, myself included, have a signature item that they wear when selling books or speaking on panels. For me, it's a plaid scally cap. A friend of mine has a kutte with all kinds of patches sewn onto it.

Another author I know wears kilts. There are two reasons you would want to consider some flair. The first is it helps to distinguish you from everyone else. If you are speaking on a panel and someone wants to find you after to speak to you, they have your flair to find you with. Flair makes you easy to identify.

There's a country singer you might have heard of, Dolly Parton. Did you know the Dolly we see is a character she plays in public? I've heard that when she goes out in public as herself, no one recognizes her. She based this character on the 'town tramp' from the town she grew up in. Like Dolly, flair can also help put you in your author persona. As authors, we have to decide how much of ourselves to share with the public. It can work like a mask, subconsciously signaling that it's time to do business or activate that extroverted persona.

Paneling

I've mentioned paneling a couple of times up to this point. Let's look at if paneling is right for you. Paneling will affect your reach. You aren't going to be at your table for about an hour for each panel you do. This will reduce your reach by twelve for each panel you participate in, right? Not so fast. You'll be speaking to people while you're paneling as well. How many? That depends on how many people show up. I've done panels that no one showed up for and I've had standing room only. When you do a panel, you should take a book and some business cards with you. You will have an opportunity to introduce yourself at the beginning of the panel. You can show a book or two and give a very brief description. Let's assume that the average panel room at a mid-sized convention will hold thirty people. Let's also assume the panels you do average out to half full. That's fifteen people you could pitch to for an hour time investment per panel. That's three higher than you could pitch to if you stayed at your table... or is it?

The truth is, there are diminishing rewards to paneling. If you are paneling in the writer's track then the same people will come to writer's track panels over and over. Your first panel will be fresh faces, you next will have some people returning, if you do five panels over a weekend by the fifth you can expect to have seen everyone in the audience at least once. It may be possible get around this by paneling with multiple tracks.

Will it be worth it? That depends how well you panel. The more outgoing, talkative, and likeable you are, the better response you will have and the more books you can sell. The issue is there will be other authors on the panel as well. It's not just you. A best-case scenario is the speakers feed off of each other with a lively back and forth that is entertaining, and informative. It's much too common for authors to let their nerves get the best of them and just talk. They go off on tangents or give bad advice in an authoritative, confident way.

A panel I was on recently was about research. One of the authors went off on a tangent about how if you wanted to write a Pegasus you have to figure out what the anatomy of a Pegasus would be if they really existed. If you don't, you can't write one. I hope you can feel my eyes rolling to the back of my skull.

If the audience likes you and feels you have contributed well, some of them might buy your books. If you're socially awkward and quiet, chances are you aren't going to make any sales from paneling. If it's worth it will depend on how well you spoke and the impression you made on the audience. It can pay off and it can pay off big, but most of the time, if there are good crowds around, I'd prefer to stay at my table.

If you are going to panel, and you should for the experience, let me give you a tip no one else will tell you. There's nothing wrong with not having anything else to add to the conversation. If you're the last to speak, it's okay to say that the other panelists did a great job covering the topic and you don't have anything to add. A good moderator will have different people go first for each question, so you can make it up on the next question.

The Great Debate: Stand or Sit

I've sold books standing and I've sold them sitting. I haven't noticed a difference either way. I think the best advice depends on who's doing the selling. For example, John Hartness is a sitter. The self-proclaimed redneck Hagrid is a big dude. Many readers are introverts that might be intimidated by a burly man with a beard rising from a stack of books like a dragon from its horde. To appear less intimidating, he sits. On the other side, if you're a petite build and disappear behind your display when sitting, then you should definitely stand. If you're like me, somewhere in the middle, I think standing lets you connect with customers better. That being said, I think this is so far down on the list of things to consider in book sales that its effects are negligible for anyone who isn't on the extremes.

Outdoor Specific Equipment

The most common space size, for indoor and outdoor events, is ten by ten. This is also the standard size for vendor tents. I recommend, and use, a Eurmax brand tent. There are cheaper options available but I like the Eurmax quality. Whatever tent you choose, make sure you get one where the poles go straight up. The poles of cheaper recreational tents slant inwards, leaving you with a canopy of roughly seven by seven feet of coverage. This may by fine to begin with, but as your catalog and display grows, you'll be glad for those vertical poles with the extra square feet. Vendor tents also have sidewalls. You can put them up to get out of the sun or protect against wind and rain.

Speaking of wind, you will need tent weights. The tent weights that come with the Eurmax tents are bags you fill with sand. I made custom weights out of PVC pipe filled with sand. The bags are good but they tend to leak if they tip over. I attach the PVC tubes to the legs of the tent with Velcro strips. You don't have to make custom weights, though. Barbells and Velcro work just as well. If you're not on pavement, and the venue allows it, you can use spikes to secure the tent to the ground. This is the most secure option. If you use them, make sure you have a hammer to drive and pull up the stakes.

As far as a table, if you're only going to have one, get a standard eight-foot folding table. The reason being, even when you do an event that provides a table, an eight foot is the most common size. The last thing you will need is a chair. A simple folding camp chair will do the job. I have a hammock chair that is very comfortable and attracts a lot of attention on its own. My favorite chair is a "tall director's chair." The seat is the same height as the table. It has a footrest and back support. Many come with a folding shelf and a side pocket for storage. The added height means you can be seen as if you were standing while remaining seated. The best of both worlds.

Part Three: Connecting with Readers and Making Sales

Passive vs Active Sales Style

Most authors don't do well at events. It's not their books, it's not their display, and it's not the event. It's that they choose a passive sales style. By that, I mean they sit behind their table and wait for someone to step up and ask them about their book. With a proper display, you will have people stop by to inquire about your book. If you want to do well at events, step out of your comfort zone and adopt an active sales style. That means engaging people that show interest in your work but wouldn't otherwise stop. It will take some practice to be comfortable engaging random people passing by, but it's worth it.

You might wonder how many more sales you can expect using an active sales strategy. I did a test. I went to one of my regular events, set up my display, and sat there. Comparing the numbers afterwards showed me that my sales were five times higher when I engaged a potential customer rather than waiting to be engaged. With that in mind, let's take a look at how to do it properly.

Let's Talk About Fishing

If you're going fishing, you need bait. Two bait options you can use are live bait and lures. Live bait is the things fish want to eat. Worms, crickets, minnows, all the things a fish can't wait to take a bite out of. You don't have to do anything with live bait, but put it on a hook, throw it in the water, and wait. The fish do the work. A retractable banner is an example of live bait. Someone walking by sees it, wants to know more, and comes to the table. You absolutely should use live bait in your display.

Lures are artificial. They fool the fish into thinking it's live bait and it takes work from the angler to sell the illusion. The fish doesn't know the difference until it takes a bite. Once they do, they learn their mistake and try to get away. It's no different with your customers. Anything you put on your table to attract attention that isn't directly related to your books is a lure. It brings people in under false pretense. A trick. Once people realize they've been tricked their instinct will be the same as the fish, get away as fast as possible. This leads us to the last thing that I feel strongly about.

Don't Put Candy on Your Table

If you search the internet for tips on selling books in person, half the results you find will tell you to put candy on your table. The idea behind it is that people walking by will see a candy dish on your table and come over to grab a piece. Now that they're at your table, you have an opportunity to talk to them about your book.

Candy is a lure. People that come to your table because of a candy dish want candy, not books. You have to buy the candy, carry it around, and have some way to display it. I'm not saying that you won't make sales from candy, I'm just saying I've never met anyone who has. When I see someone at an event with candy on their table, I ask them how it performed for them. I have yet to run into a success story. Luckily, there's a better way to fish.

Cast Net

You don't need bait at all to fish if you use a cast net. For anyone who isn't familiar, a cast net is a weighted net on a rope. You throw it into the water, it traps the fish, then you pull them in with the rope. Of course, you don't know what you're going to get until you get the net on shore and take a look. You get some fish you want and some you don't. You throw the ones you don't want back and try again.

Any fans of Lost out there? Remember the scene where Jin, played by Daniel Dae Kim, is supposed to be fishing and we see him sitting on a rock throwing stuff in the water? Ana, played by Michelle Rodriguez, sees him sitting instead of fishing. She goes over and tells him that he should be fishing. He can't just sit around like a lazy bum all day and expect to eat. Jin sits there quietly, throwing something in the water while she berates him. Then he stands up, throws a cast net, and pulls in a bunch of fish. Jin had been throwing sea urchin in the water to attract fish, then used the cast net to catch them.

That's how this sales strategy works. We set up a display designed to attract the right people. Instead of waiting for them to come up to the table, we engage them first. Throw our net out and see what we catch.

Not everyone will buy, of course, but some will, and you'll make many more sales than if you sit and wait for them to come to you.

Just as many readers are introverted, many writers are as well. If you aren't willing to speak to people to bring them to your booth, you'll have to stick to a passive sales style. In that case, the largest event you can do will be the best, since it will give you the most people walking by your display. If you're interested in increasing your sales by a multiple of five with an active sales style, then the largest event isn't always best. That's why in the events we looked at earlier the mid-sized event was the most profitable. You don't need tens of thousands of people to walk by your booth to have a good day. Let's look at an active sales style in action.

Don't Try to Sell Books

Yes, you read that right. I know, this is a book about selling books and now I'm telling you to not to try to sell books. Let me explain. I am a very low-pressure sales kind of guy. I can honestly say I don't care if someone I speak to buys my book or not. When you're starting out, it's easy to focus on the number of books sold. If you do that, you will get frustrated when things don't go your way. That frustration is going to come through in your interactions and make sales harder to get. You want to portray an air of confidence, not desperation.

Instead, look at an event as a way to get the word out about your work. It's an opportunity to build a relationship with a potential fan. If people like you, they are more likely to buy your book, sign up for your newsletter, or pass your business card to a friend. How many high-pressure sales interactions have you had that left you with a positive feeling about the salesperson? If you speak to one hundred people at an event, that's one hundred people that yesterday didn't know you existed. If they come away from that interaction with a positive impression of you, that's a win. Don't be a salesperson, be an author telling people about your book. Don't focus on sales, the sales will come.

Three Seconds to Contact

When I'm at my table, I am constantly scanning the crowd. I'm looking for anyone interested in my display. How do I know? They look at it. If I see someone looking at anything on my display, I count to three. If my display holds their interest for my count, I engage them. To be fair, it's not actually three seconds. "Three seconds to contact" just has a nice ring to it. It's closer to a second and a half.

I ask them a question. Some people advise against close-ended questions that can be answered with a "yes" or "no". I don't think it makes a difference. Open-ended questions are more of a high-pressure tactic, as it forces the person to engage or ignore you. They don't have easy answers. Examples would be, "What's your favorite suspense novel?" or "If you could be any supernatural creature, what would you be?"

We shouldn't be using social pressure to coerce people into talking to us. If someone isn't interested in what I have, then I want them to keep moving. Time you spend talking to them could be spent finding someone who would love your work.

I mostly use close-ended questions. What question depends on what kind of event it is. If I'm at an author event, everyone will know that the person behind the book wrote it. Otherwise, it's a good idea to fit that into your question. One of the questions I use is, "Can I tell you about the urban fantasy series I wrote?" The "I wrote" is the most important part of the question. They will be more likely to speak to you if they know you're the author and not just a random person trying to sell them something. They may make an excuse or just say "no" and that's fine. If they don't want to talk to me, I don't want to talk to them either. I'm just casting my net and seeing what I catch. More often than not, they will come over to your table.

The most natural thing to do is throw out a greeting. "Hello!" I still find myself doing this from time to time. It's the most common thing people do when trying to engage a potential customer. It doesn't work. At one literary festival I was attending, I walked through the vendor area.

A woman at a booth said, "hello", as I walked by.

"Hello," I said, and kept walking.

She wasn't ready to give up yet. "How are you?"

I looked at the book on the table. It didn't grab my attention.

"I'm fine," I said.

By that time, I was gone because I never stopped walking.

I've thought a lot about this interaction. If she had started with, "Can I tell you about my book?" I would have stopped. I don't think I would have bought it. It didn't look like something I normally read, but who knows? Worst case, I would know who she is now.

The more you do events, the more comfortable you will be speaking to strangers. It does get boring saying the same things over and over. Sometimes the boredom gets the best of me and I mix things up for the novelty. One of my favorite things to say in this situation is, "I have that wereotter book you were looking for." This isn't something I recommend for your main line, but it's fun to see people's reactions. I don't use this line on just anyone. I've learned to spot the people this is most effective on.

I heard of one author that writes comedy that sometimes says, "Come over here and give me your damn money." You know what's crazy? It works... for him. He's learned to spot the people this line will work on. The author that told me about this saw it working and tried it for himself with very different results. There isn't a magic phrase you can say that will bring people over and make them buy your book. What works for one person won't work for another. It will take practice to find out what your audience responds to, what bait they prefer.

Developing a Good Pitch

Before you can deliver your pitch, you have to have one. It's common for a new author without an established pitch to just talk about their book. They stand there droning on and on and end up talking themselves out of a sale. If you find yourself with diarrhea of the mouth, I can promise you that potential reader is going to think they made a mistake talking to you. They'll be too busy looking for the first exit they can get to listen to what you're saying.

A good pitch is a short pitch. One minute or less. My pitch was fifty-seven seconds. You may hear that's too long, that a pitch should only be thirty seconds. To that I say, I sell a lot of books. A sixty-second pitch that works is better than a thirty-second pitch that doesn't. You need to describe the key elements of your story to intrigue a potential reader into buying it. It's no small feat to do this in a concise manner. Chances are you are too close to your book to do this well on the first try. You'll need to do some trial and error. You're going to have to play around with it to figure out what works. Short and sweet is the name of the game. I moved away from my fifty-seven second pitch to a five second pitch. I discovered it's all I need to make sales. Not everyone can get away with a pitch that short.

Before your event, spend some time thinking about what you're going to say. Try writing it out and timing yourself to make sure you get it under sixty seconds. Practice it with friends, family, and in the mirror. I deliver my pitch thousands of times a year. Even when I was using my fifty-seven second pitch, I didn't have to think about it anymore. My mind wandered about what I'm having for lunch while my mouth ran through the words on its own. You need your pitch to be second nature. This will come with practice.

Confidence

Confidence while delivering a pitch is just as important as what you say. I believe in the quality of my work. I didn't always though. As a new author, I was filled with doubts. What if they buy it and hate it? What if I get bad reviews? I've had people walk up to my table to tell me they got my book and enjoyed it, or asking when the next book will be out. Positive feedback from readers put those feelings to rest. One woman got the ebook and liked it so much she came back for a signed paperback. The point is, if you don't believe it's any good, no one else will either. Be confident about your work and you will instill confidence in a potential buyer.

Once at an event I was in the middle of a pitch when a woman walked up and started whispering to my partner. That was strange. When I finished my partner told me that the woman was Katlyn. She found my book at a used bookstore, thought it looked interesting, and bought it. She didn't read fantasy but for whatever reason, that day, she got it. She read it in two days, and now, because of my book, fantasy is her favorite genre. I think she was nervous about talking to me, like I was some kind of celebrity. I went out from behind the table and took a picture with her. It meant so much to me to hear that story. Having positive interactions with fans will put any insecurities you have to rest.

My Pitch

The pitch I settled on when I had one book out was something like this:

This novel is set in north Georgia and is about Obie. This is Obie (I say pointing to him on the retractable banner) he's a wereotter and a keeper of the Earth Mother. Demons come through portals from other words, eat people and cause problems, and it's the Keepers job to hunt them down. In book one, something is using magic to attack the Earth Mother. She's not going to stand for that, so she tells him that if he can't put a stop to it quick, she's going to handle it herself. That means floods, earthquakes, tornadoes basically kill everyone in the region to get rid of the one thing that's messing with her. He has to figure out what's doing it and how to stop it before she gets impatient enough to handle it herself."

Looking at that pitch, I know it could be better, but it worked, so it stopped evolving there. Now that I have the trilogy complete, and a few years more experience, my pitch is, "This is my urban fantasy trilogy about a wereotter hunting demons in north Georgia." I leave it at that and respond to what they say about that. It's always questioning the wereotter or North Georgia. Then I can give more details about what about what drew their attention. If they say nothing, I follow up after a few seconds with, "If you're interested, feel free to pick it up, read the back, or flip through it."

After the Pitch

Whatever pitch you settle on, deliver it and stop talking. Just shut up. It's their turn to speak. Only one of four things will happen a that point.

1. They will say they don't want it. No problem, give them a card and move on.

2. They will ask a follow-up question that you will answer as briefly as possible. Avoid rambling. The two most common questions I get are "How much is it?" And "Is it Christian?" What can I say, I live in the bible belt.

3. They will pick up a copy and look inside. Most of the people that pick up a book will buy it.

4. They will buy it. Hooray!

Keep engaging potential readers and pitching and you will have sales.

High-pressure sales tactics

I'm against high-pressure tactics. Let's take a look at some I've heard of authors doing.

If you look at tips online about developing a pitch, you will be told to include a call to action. "Buy it today!" I don't advocate a call to action in an in-person context. As I said before, I don't ask anyone to buy my book. The closest I come is letting them know they are free to pick it up if they want to, no pressure.

At one event, I spotted someone I wanted to engage and asked, "Can I tell you about the urban fantasy series I write?"

"I don't have any money," he replied.

I was having a rough day at this event, so I wasn't as friendly as I intended. "I didn't ask you for money, I asked you to listen."

"Okay, I'll listen," he said sheepishly.

I should have said, "That's okay, I'm just trying to get the word out about my books." I'm not perfect though. I still mess up at this and that's okay. When we mess up, we learn from it and do better next time.

I delivered my pitch and went right into handing him a card with my usual request to pass it on to someone that might like it.

I said in option three of After the Sale that if someone picks up a book, they will often buy it. Some authors will force this by handing a copy of the book to the potential buyer. It will increase sales, but you shouldn't do it.

Another tactic is to over-inflate claims about your work. "It's like Stephen King but better." No. Just no. You should try to find your success by dragging your colleges through the dirt. A reader will be rightfully skeptical of these claims. If someone says something like this to me, I'm not only not buying their book, I don't see myself working with that author in the future.

We stay away from high-pressure tactics because they are a short-term strategy. We want a potential reader to have a positive impression of us as people. The goal is to turn them into fans that will buy the books we haven't written yet and talk to their friends about how wonderful we are. Let's look at a hypothetical that I think will drive the point home.

Let's say you used a high-pressure tactic to sell a book. That customer has company that evening. Your book is sitting on the coffee table.

The guest sees it and asks, "What's this?"

What is your buyer going to say?

With high pressure sales it may be something like, "Oh, I was at an event today and I met the author. He was really pushy. I didn't even want it, but ended up buying it just to get away from him."

If you made a good impression the reader might respond with "I met the author at an event today. He was really nice and he wrote this book about a wereotter. I'll let you know how it is when I finish it."

If your buyer has a negative impression of you, what do you think the chances are they are going to read your book? We need people to read our work and recommend it to others to build our business. Making ten dollars isn't worth alienating a reader.

They say they want it... What now?

Once they commit to buying, the next thing I ask is, "Cash or card?" Run the transition or make change. Once payment is complete, I say, "I've already autographed it and have a card in the book. I'd be happy to personalize it if you like."

Some authors assume that because they bought a book, they must want their name with a personalized message in it. They automatically ask what their name is so they can sign the book to them. About half the people I sell to don't want it personalized. By pre-signing and asking about personalization, I can complete the transaction faster, get on to my next sale, and give the customer exactly what they want.

Last, I ask them if they want a bag. I use a clear "die cut handle bag". I purchase clear bags because other people can see the book in them. As your new fan walks around the event, other people will see that they bought your book. When those people make it around to your display, they already know that people are willing to pay for your work. Your job just got a little easier.

You don't have to provide bags. It's not expected. I didn't have them at first, but I think it's a nice touch and worth the potential advertising. My bags cost around four cents each. That's a cost I'm willing to eat for someone that buys. I really don't like using plastic bags, but I haven't found another cost-effective option. You could go with a brown paper bag with a handle. The issue is you lose the potential advertising. You could order custom printed bags with your book cover on them or print something out on a sticker to affix to the bag. These options add cost to an already more expensive bag.

If you use the clear bags and they buy more than one book, put the books back to back when you put them inside, so no matter which way the bag is facing, a cover is visible.

The Downside

While this strategy works, it's hard. It means you have to be "on" for hours on end, constantly talking to someone. For many introverted authors, this may seem impossible. It gets easier. That being said, by the end of a day of sales, I'm spent. I want a quiet room to disappear into. This is exacerbated by a multi-day event. I don't think I've ever been more drained than after a four-day event that I spoke to hundreds of people at. If talking to people is a draining experience for you, then do your best with it and if you need a few minutes here and there to recharge your batteries, take them. There's nothing wrong with taking care of yourself. It can be easy when you sit down for a little break to stay that way. You will lose some of your momentum from sitting down, and it may feel like starting over for the day when you decide to start pitching again. Sometimes it's easier to keep going.

After the Event

You should keep records of your events. It's nice to be able to look back and see how many sales you've made. It's also useful to see how you did when deciding if you want to do that event again. After all, the best way to tell how good an event is, is to do it. It will also come in handy at the end of the year for tax time. I keep a spreadsheet with all my profits and expenses that I try to keep updated throughout the year.

While you have a little cash on hand, there're two things you should do right away. Pay your sales tax, if required, and order more books. It can take weeks for your books to arrive. Look at the events you have planned and how many books you will need so you can get them early. It can take up to a month in some cases to receive your books after you order them.

I'm always skeptical when I see author's posts about selling out at shows. I've sold out of a title a few times. Every time I did it was because I had low inventory going in. If you plan correctly, you won't run out of books.

Troubleshooting

You did an event and you didn't do so well. Let's see if we can figure out what the problem is so the next one is better.

No One Was Around

Unfortunately, you had a bad event. The single biggest factor that determines your success is attendance. If the event doesn't draw a crowd, you don't have anything to work with. The only thing you can do is avoid that event in the future. It's happened to me before, and it will again. Unfortunately, this is just part of it. If you find yourself in this situation, you can spend the downtime talking to other vendors and making connections. If you have your computer or a Bluetooth keyboard you can spend time writing your next book. Think about what you can do to get the most out of that event besides sales.

Alternately, if the event had good attendance but people aren't making it back to you, then you just have a bad spot. The spot you get is luck of the draw. I don't know how events place their vendors, but no matter what, some spots will be better than others. If you find yourself in a low traffic area, take a walk and see if there are any vacant spots in a better area. If you find one, ask to move. It will be a pain, but it's better than sitting on your thumbs the whole time. I've always found events accommodating in this scenario.

At one event I did, I was assigned a space in the back corner facing the wall. Next to no one came back that far. The autograph area was on the other side, so the people that did come by were on their way to their scheduled signings and weren't stopping. I couldn't move spaces, so I had to make due. At times, I would walk out to scout who was headed in my direction. I was also a little more aggressive with my casts. What I did to make the best of the situation was to engage people who didn't look at my display but were just in proximity of the table. I had a much higher proportion of people decline to speak to me. It was a rough weekend, but I still left with a profit.

At another show, I had an author table in a back corner. People only came by on their way to panels, so sales were slow. After an abysmal Friday and Saturday, I scouted the area Sunday morning and found a vacant table right up front. There had been someone at it up to that point. I asked to move and was given the okay. It was night and day. I did so many sales on Sunday that I was happy with what I had made by the end of the day. If I had stayed in the back corner, it would have been one of my worst events ever.

<u>People Aren't Looking at Your Display</u>

This is pretty straight forward. You display isn't appealing. It doesn't have something to attract people's attention or what it does have isn't working. You could be at an event where a large percentage of the fan base isn't your target audience. If you don't have a banner, consider getting one. If you write Science Fiction or Fantasy you could consider wearing a costume related to your work. Dress up as one of the characters. This will only work if people have a vague idea of what you are, though. I know of one author who writes high fantasy. She works renaissance fairs and shows up to all her events in a suit of armor. That will attract some major attention. Don't be afraid to think outside the box to find a creative solution. Be careful though. Whatever you do, make sure it doesn't cost so much that you'll have to spend months of sales to make your money back.

<u>People Are Coming to Your Table But They're Not Buying</u>

This indicates a problem with your book or your pitch. If you're not selling anything, it's probably both. A good pitch can sell a less than ideal book, but no matter how good the book looks, if your pitch is bad, you will scare people off. I've changed the cover of my first book twice before I got something that worked the way I wanted it to. If you're just starting out, you can expect to have a rough go of it. Sales is a skill, and it will take practice to develop.

Start off by doing small local events. They're a great way to practice without a steep price tag. If you know an author that does well, ask to team up for an event. If they are selling and you're not, ask them what you're doing wrong, and be open to the criticism. That doesn't mean you should take their advice, but it will give you some things to consider about what you could be doing better.

Real Numbers

Now let's look at some actual events and see how this system pre-formed. I'll be providing my numbers and comparing how the formula holds up. Bob McGough, who wrote the forward for this book, was kind enough to let me share some of his numbers as well. He posts sales numbers on his blog after events if you care to check it out.

<u>Event One:</u>

This is a large four-day convention. I had a table in the vendor hall.

The results of the formula break down like this:

2040 Minutes (34 Hours selling hours)/5(turnaround time) = 408 Reach

408 (Reach) x .33(sales rate) = 135 Potential Sales

135(Potential Sales) – 15% = 115 Expected Sales

How I did:

Complete Trilogy Sold: 50 $1960

Petrified 2 $34

Other 30 $295

The trilogy messes with my book numbers a little. It has three books in it, and I earn the profit of three books so let's multiply its number by three to compare evenly.

Total Books Sold: 152 $1994

Total Sales: $2289

Sales Rate: 37%

Event Two:

This is a two-day convention Bob did. He had an author ally table.

The results of the formula:

1080 Minutes (18 Hours selling hours)/5(turnaround time) = 216 Reach

216 (Reach) x .33(sales rate) = 71 Potential Sales

71(Potential Sales) – 15% = 61 Expected Sales

How he did:

Omnibus one sales: 8

Omnibus two sales: 5

Book one sales: 7

Southern Saudade Sales: 8

Ultimate Bundle: 1 (Seven Book Bundle)

Other 10

Total Books Sold: 61

Total Sales: $754

Sales Rate: 33%

Here, Bob sold exactly to the Formula. His catalog is much larger than mine, seven books total and two omnibus editions.

Event Three:

This is a small two-day event. I had an author ally table.

The results of the formula break down like this:

840 Minutes (14 Hours selling hours)/5(turnaround time) = 168 Reach

168 (Reach) x .33(sales rate) = 55 Potential Sales

55(Potential Sales) – 15% = 47 Expected Sales

How I did:

Complete Trilogy Sold: 17 $646

Petrified 7 $119

Other 16 $132

Adjusting for the trilogy:

Total Books Sold: 58 $765

Total Sales: $897

Sales Rate: 35%

As you can see, I outperformed the formula in this event. The omnibus goes a long way to making events more profitable since it's so easy to upsell.

Event Four:

This is a medium-sized three day convention where Bob was sharing space with four other authors in the vendor hall.

The results of the formula:

1380 Minutes (23 Hours selling hours)/5(turnaround time) = 276 Reach

276 (Reach) x .2(sales rate) = 55 Potential Sales

55(Potential Sales) – 15% = 47 Expected Sales

How he did:

Omnibus one sales: 8

Omnibus two sales: 3

Book one sales: 14

Southern Saudades Sales: 0

Ultimate Bundle: 0 (Seven Book Bundle)

Other 8

Total Books Sold: 47

Total Sales: $700

Sales Rate: 17%

Since there were five authors sharing a space, I lowered the sales rate from 33% to 20%. This is due to the increased competition the other authors provide. As you can see, Bob again nailed the Expected Sales to the book.

You can see from these numbers that breaking $700 for an event becomes normal. I had an event recently where I was disappointed by a $700 event. It's not that I was unhappy with the total earnings but the event was slow over all, so it had so much more potential. I know authors with large catalogues and excellent displays that will break $5,000 at the right events. This is still something I'm building my catalog to work my way to, but I'll get there. My most profitable event to date was a little over $2,600.

Conclusion

There you have it, a complete strategy for selling books in person that will work, if you get out there and hustle. It may seem impossible to make thousands of dollars over a weekend selling books in person. If you're intimidated by any aspect of personal sales, I understand. I have good news! You only need to sell one book to be successful. I say this because if you can sell one book you can sell a hundred or a thousand. This is a great mentality to have. It takes the pressure off when you're starting. You only have to sell *one* book. Then, after you've sold that one, sell one more. That's how you eat an elephant. One bite at a time.

Event Checklist

Outdoor Events:

- Tent
- Sidewalls
- Tent Weights
- Table
- Chair

Indoor Events:

- Tablecloths
- Book Stands
- Point of Sale System
- Change

- Battery

- Charging Cables

- Books

- Signage

- Newsletter Signup

- Pens

- Banner

- Business Cards

- Bags

- Cooler with food and drinks

About the Author

Message from the Author

I hope you enjoyed my work! If you did, please consider leaving a review on Amazon, Goodreads, and referring this book to a friend! You can keep up with what's going on with me at authorbenmeeks. com, by signing up for my newsletter, and following me on Facebook (authorbenmeeks), and Instagram (authorbenmeeks).

Ben grew up in Dahlonega, the biggest small town in the North Georgia mountains. He spent his childhood appreciating nature and, as he grew older, benefited from a wide variety of unusual and exciting experiences. Ben traveled internationally, including Europe and India. He participated in, and won, a martial arts competition, was hit by a ricocheting bullet, and was in a high-speed car chase. He also received a late-night phone call from the secret service, who he hung up on.

Ben appreciates fantasy and sci-fi in all forms, with a particular fondness for shifters. He excels at creative, outside the box thinking combined with a drive toward realism that gives his work a unique feel. He is the author of the award-winning urban fantasy trilogy, *The Keeper Chronicles.*

www.ingramcontent.com/pod-product-compliance
Lightning Source LLC
Chambersburg PA
CBHW071504210326
41597CB00018B/2686